INSIDE THE NFL

LOS ANGELES CHARGERS

by Charlie Beattie

Abdo & Daughters
MIDDLE GRADE NONFICTION

An imprint of Abdo Publishing
abdobooks.com

ABDOBOOKS.COM

Published by Abdo Publishing, a division of ABDO, PO Box 398166, Minneapolis, Minnesota 55439.

Printed in China.
052025
092025

THIS BOOK CONTAINS RECYCLED MATERIALS

Cover Photos: Courtney Culbreath/Getty Images Sport/Getty Images (Justin Herbert); Matt A. Brown/Icon Sportswire/Getty Images (Junior Seau)
Interior Photos: Harry How/Getty Images Sport/Getty Images, 4-5, 8 (bottom), 61 (bottom right); Chris Williams/Icon Sportswire/Getty Images, 6; Lynne Sladky/AP Images, 7; Kyusung Gong/AP Images, 8 (top); Kevork Djansezian/Getty Images Sport/Getty Images, 9; Abdo Publishing, 10-11; Los Angeles Examiner/USC Libraries/Corbis Historical/Getty Images, 12-13; Bettmann/Getty Images, 14, 16; Vic Stein/Getty Images Sport/Getty Images, 15; Charles Aqua Viva/Getty Images Sport/Getty Images, 17, 18, 20, 24-25, 60 (top right); AP Images, 19, 30, 32, 33; James Drake/Getty Images Sport/Getty Images, 21; George Long/Sports Illustrated/Getty Images, 22-23; James Flores/Getty Images Sport/Getty Images, 26, 60 (top left); Chuck Solomon/AP Images, 27; Al Messerschmidt Archive/AP Images, 28, 60 (bottom); Focus on Sport/Getty Images, 29; Focus on Sport/Getty Images Sport/Getty Images, 31; George Gojkovich/Getty Images Sport/Getty Images, 34-35; Keith Srakocic/AP Images, 36; G. Newman Lowrance/AP Images, 37, 44-45; Paul Spinelli/NFL Photos/AP Images, 38; Ed Zurga/AP Images, 39; Jeff Haynes/AFP/Getty Images, 40; Phil Sandlin/AP Images, 41, 61 (bottom left); Stephen Dunn/Allsport/Getty Images Sport/Getty Images, 42, 43; Paul Spinelli/AP Images, 46; Denis Poroy/AP Images, 47, 50, 61 (top); Jeff Gross/Getty Images Sport/ Getty Images, 48; Chris Carlson/AP Images, 49; Ezra Shaw/Getty Images Sport/Getty Images, 51; Scott Cunningham/Getty Images Sport/Getty Images, 53; Peter Read Miller/AP Images, 54; Peter Joneleit/AP Images, 55, 63; Shutterstock Images, 56; Ryan Kang/Getty Images Sport/Getty Images, 57; Ronald Martinez/Getty Images Sport/Getty Images, 58

Editor: Rebecca Higgins
Series Designer: Laura Graphenteen
Production Designer: Laura Kuchar

Library of Congress Control Number: 2024948507

Publisher's Cataloging-in-Publication Data

Names: Beattie, Charlie, author.
Title: Los Angeles Chargers / by Charlie Beattie
Description: Minneapolis, Minnesota: Abdo Publishing, 2026 | Series: Inside the NFL | Includes online resources and index.
Identifiers: ISBN 9781098296797 (lib. bdg.) | ISBN 9798384919315 (ebook)
Subjects: LCSH: Los Angeles Chargers (Football team)--Juvenile literature. | National Football League--Juvenile literature. | Football teams--Juvenile literature. | American football--Juvenile literature.
Classification: DDC 796.333--dc23

CONTENTS

Los Angeles Chargers quarterback Justin Herbert looks for an open receiver in September 2020.

CHAPTER 1

HERBERT ARRIVES

Justin Herbert took his spot 5 yards behind the center for a shotgun snap. It was Week 2 of the 2020 National Football League (NFL) season. The rookie quarterback stared down a Kansas City Chiefs defense that had claimed the most recent Super Bowl title.

Many rookies would have been overwhelmed in this situation, but Herbert looked calm as he drove his Los Angeles Chargers down the field. The quarterback had already completed two passes totaling 51 yards. Then, on first-and-goal from Kansas City's 4-yard line, the 22-year-old Herbert was ready to finish the drive. With millions of people watching along from around the country, Herbert didn't have time to consider that he wasn't even supposed to be playing in this game in the first place.

THE NEW KID

Herbert threw for 10,541 yards and 95 touchdowns at Oregon. Both totals were the second most in the school's history.

For 14 years, Chargers fans were used to seeing Philip Rivers as starting quarterback. The record-setting passer had joined the team in 2004 and led the then–San Diego Chargers to many successful seasons. The Chargers moved to Los Angeles in 2017 and made the playoffs the next year, but then they struggled to a 5–11 finish in 2019. After that season, Rivers met with the team and agreed to move on. The Chargers planned to rebuild their roster with younger players.

Los Angeles selected Herbert with the sixth pick in the 2020 draft. The 6-foot-6, 236-pound athlete possessed a powerful arm combined with a strong running ability. Herbert had everything NFL teams look for in a quarterback. While most high draft picks play right away, the Chargers had other plans. The team already had respected veteran backup Tyrod Taylor on its roster. Los Angeles wanted Herbert to watch from the sideline and learn the professional game while Taylor played. Then the rookie would take over.

Taylor guided the Chargers to a 16–13 road win against the Cincinnati Bengals in Week 1. However, the 31-year-old Taylor cracked two of his ribs during the game. The team hoped he could play through the injury. But just before kickoff of the Chargers' home opener against the Chiefs the next week, Taylor started experiencing pain. Instead of taking the field, he was rushed to the hospital. To fans' surprise, Herbert came out for the Chargers' first play. The young quarterback promptly drove Los Angeles 75 yards and put them in position to score.

Herbert, *right*, started the 2020 season backing up veteran Tyrod Taylor, *left*.

Herbert (10) scans the Kansas City defense before a snap.

PAYDIRT

As the Chargers lined up at the Chiefs' 4, offensive coordinator Shane Steichen called for a pass. Herbert stood under center and scanned the field. After taking the snap, he faked a handoff to running back Joshua Kelley. The rookie quarterback rolled to his right.

All his receivers were covered. After a slight hesitation, Herbert sprinted toward

The Associated Press named Herbert the NFL's 2020 Offensive Rookie of the Year.

the goal line. Just inside the pylon, he crossed the line for the game's first touchdown. Then Herbert was blasted by Kansas City defensive end Michael Danna. The quarterback was sent tumbling out of bounds.

Herbert popped back up and was immediately surrounded by cheering teammates. Though the Chargers eventually fell to the Chiefs in overtime, Herbert threw for more than 300 yards and a passing touchdown in his thrilling debut. He became the third NFL quarterback to rack up 300 yards passing and rush for a touchdown in his first game. The only other quarterbacks to accomplish the feat were NFL legend Otto Graham and former Most Valuable Player (MVP) Cam Newton. When Week 3 rolled around, few were surprised when Herbert jogged onto the field as the starter.

ROOKIE RECORD

Opponents feared Justin Herbert's dangerous arm. During a Week 16 matchup against the Denver Broncos, the quarterback threw a 9-yard touchdown pass to running back Austin Ekeler. It was Herbert's 28th touchdown pass of the year and broke the record for rookies. He added three more a week later competing against the Chiefs. Herbert's rookie record reached 31 touchdown passes.

Herbert celebrates a touchdown pass during the 2020 season with receiver Mike Williams.

NFL TEAMS MAP

NFC

NFC EAST

- DALLAS COWBOYS
- NEW YORK GIANTS
- PHILADELPHIA EAGLES
- WASHINGTON COMMANDERS

NFC WEST

- ARIZONA CARDINALS
- LOS ANGELES RAMS
- SAN FRANCISCO 49ERS
- SEATTLE SEAHAWKS

NFC NORTH

- CHICAGO BEARS
- DETROIT LIONS
- GREEN BAY PACKERS
- MINNESOTA VIKINGS

NFC SOUTH

- ATLANTA FALCONS
- CAROLINA PANTHERS
- NEW ORLEANS SAINTS
- TAMPA BAY BUCCANEERS

AFC

AFC EAST

- BUFFALO BILLS
- MIAMI DOLPHINS
- NEW ENGLAND PATRIOTS
- NEW YORK JETS

AFC WEST

- DENVER BRONCOS
- KANSAS CITY CHIEFS
- LAS VEGAS RAIDERS
- LOS ANGELES CHARGERS

AFC NORTH

- BALTIMORE RAVENS
- CINCINNATI BENGALS
- CLEVELAND BROWNS
- PITTSBURGH STEELERS

AFC SOUTH

- HOUSTON TEXANS
- INDIANAPOLIS COLTS
- JACKSONVILLE JAGUARS
- TENNESSEE TITANS

From left, owner Barron Hilton, head coach Sid Gillman, and general manager Frank Leahy built the early Chargers.

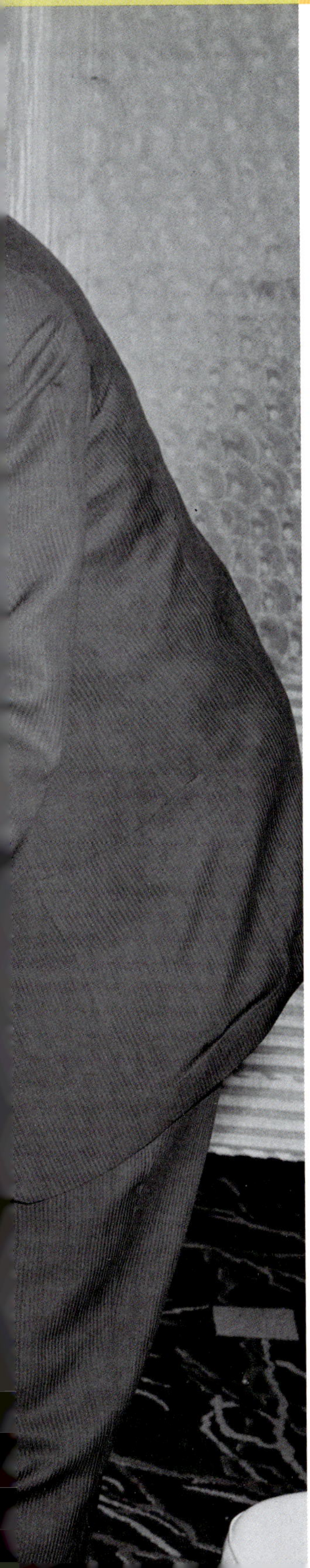

CHAPTER 2

THE BOLTS

IN THE LATE 1950S, A GROUP OF ASPIRING OWNERS GOT TOGETHER TO form the American Football League (AFL). They wanted the new league to challenge the NFL. One of the group's wealthiest owners was Barron Hilton. He was vice president of his family's hotel business. He also owned a credit card company. Hilton would lead the new league's Los Angeles franchise. He named Frank Leahy as the team's general manager.

Hilton was a fan of University of Southern California (USC) football. He liked the "Charge!" chant fans shouted at Trojans games. When Hilton and Leahy's new team took the field in 1960, it was named the Chargers.

The team's owner didn't have to go far to find a head coach. Sid Gillman had coached the NFL's Los Angeles Rams from 1955 to 1959.

Quarterback Jack Kemp (15) and offensive tackle Ron Mix (74) were two of the Chargers' early stars.

Gillman jumped at Hilton's offer to stay in Los Angeles and lead the Chargers. When Leahy had health issues and had to step down before the season, Gillman also became the Chargers' general manager.

Putting together a roster proved much tougher than finding a coach. Luckily, the Chargers caught a few breaks. Standout offensive lineman Ron Mix had just graduated from USC. Both the AFL's Boston Patriots and the NFL's Baltimore Colts picked him in their respective drafts. Mix had to decide which league to play in. The Chargers had an idea. Thinking Mix would sign with the AFL if he could stay close to home, Los Angeles traded for the lineman. That assumption proved correct when Mix signed with the AFL, giving the new team a strong player to build around.

The Chargers needed a solid quarterback for Mix to block for. They turned to Jack Kemp, who had played little in two NFL seasons before joining the Canadian Football League (CFL) in 1959. After again sitting on the bench in the CFL, the future congressman returned to the United States to sign with the Chargers.

The team also invited Paul Lowe to their training camp. The running back had excelled at Oregon State, where he became known for his quick moves. But Lowe didn't find success in the NFL. Before trying out for the Chargers, he worked in the mailroom of Hilton's credit card company. After seeing Lowe in action, Gillman knew the back could easily escape defenders and signed him.

Chargers running back Paul Lowe (23) follows Ron Mix (74) on a running play against the Houston Oilers in 1960.

SAN DIEGO BOUND

Lowe became a star for the brand-new Chargers. Running behind the future Hall of Famer Mix, Lowe rushed for 855 yards and eight touchdowns. Both totals ranked second in the AFL. The Chargers finished their first season with a 10–4 record and won the AFL's West Division.

Los Angeles was set to host the league's first championship game against the Houston Oilers. However, there was a problem. Few fans had attended the Chargers' games. They played in the 90,000-seat Los Angeles Coliseum, but there was an average of 15,000 people in the stands. Tight end Dave Kocourek joked that it would be easier for players to introduce themselves to each fan than to announce the team over the stadium's speakers. Citing Los Angeles's low attendance, the league moved the title game to Houston, where the Chargers lost 24–16. After that season, Hilton

The Chargers struggled to fill the Los Angeles Coliseum.

Along with his offensive innovations, Chargers head coach Sid Gillman, *left*, was one of the first coaches to embrace weight training for his players.

decided Los Angeles wasn't the place for his Chargers and moved the team south to San Diego.

The Chargers were immediately embraced by their new city. At the time, football was centered around running the ball. But San Diego's visionary head coach, Gillman, encouraged his quarterbacks to throw deep early and often. The result was exciting, wide-open football. "The big play comes from the pass. God bless those runners because they get you the first down, but if you want to ring the cash register, you have to pass," Gillman said.

"GOD BLESS THOSE RUNNERS BECAUSE THEY GET YOU THE FIRST DOWN, BUT IF YOU WANT TO RING THE CASH REGISTER, YOU HAVE TO PASS."

—SID GILLMAN

San Diego defensive lineman Ernie Ladd (77) played in the AFL All-Star Game each year from 1962 to 1965.

In 1961, Gillman's pass-focused offense scored 396 points, good for third place in the AFL. And on the other side of the ball, the Chargers' defense shut down opponents. San Diego forced 66 turnovers, including 49 interceptions. Both totals set pro football records. Charlie McNeil picked off nine passes and fellow safety Bob Zeman intercepted eight. After starting the season 11–0, the Chargers' offense dried up and they lost two of their final three regular-season games. But San Diego's 12–2 record was still the best in the league, and again they battled Houston for the title. The interceptions kept coming in the title game as the Chargers picked off Houston quarterback George Blanda five times. However, Kemp threw four interceptions, and the Oilers won 10–3.

CHAMPION CHARGERS

Kemp had a strong arm, but he was injured in the second game of the 1962 season. The Chargers put the quarterback on waivers and lost him to the Buffalo Bills. Rookie John Hadl became the starting quarterback. But when Hadl threw 24 interceptions in a 4–10 season, Gillman had to search for another starter. He signed veteran Tobin Rote. The quarterback had won an NFL championship with the Detroit Lions before playing the previous few seasons in Canada. When Rote returned to the United States, the Chargers won the rights to sign him in a coin flip.

Rote quickly formed a connection with 23-year-old Lance Alworth, a second-year receiver. Nicknamed "Bambi" because of his deer-like speed, Alworth caught 61 passes for more than 1,200 yards and 11 touchdowns in 1963. Rote and his receivers stretched defenses with their passing game, which opened more lanes for Lowe. The star halfback topped 1,000 rushing yards for the first time in his career. Fullback Keith Lincoln added another 826 yards.

Behind the league's best scoring offense and defense, the Chargers finished 11–3. That set up a meeting with the

In nine seasons with the Chargers, Lance Alworth averaged more than 50 catches and 1,000 yards per year.

Patriots in the championship game. During the regular season, San Diego had beaten Boston 7-6 in the Chargers' lowest-scoring game of the year.

The title game was played at San Diego's tiny Balboa Stadium. The Chargers' ground game got off to a hot start when Lincoln rushed 56 yards on the game's second play, setting up a 2-yard score for Rote. Later in the first quarter, Lincoln burst free for a 67-yard touchdown to make it 14–0. After a Boston touchdown, Lowe had to answer. Late in the first quarter he sprinted 58 yards for a score.

Alworth (19) makes a leaping catch over a Boston Patriots defender in the 1963 AFL Championship Game.

After Rote threw his first touchdown pass in the second quarter, the Chargers led 31–10. The quarterback added a 48-yard strike to Alworth in the third quarter. With the game under control, he sat out the fourth and watched Hadl complete a 25-yard touchdown pass to Lincoln and run for a

1-yard score in the 51–10 rout. Lincoln was the star of the biggest blowout in AFL championship history. Though often overshadowed by Lowe, San Diego's other star back, Lincoln, racked up 206 rushing yards in the game.

Chargers quarterback Tobin Rote throws a pass against the Buffalo Bills in the 1964 AFL title game.

A NEW HOME

The Chargers remained one of the AFL's best teams in 1964 and 1965. Hadl eventually retook the starting quarterback job. He became one of the league's top passers, with Alworth usually receiving his deep bombs. But in both seasons, the Chargers came up short in the championship game against their former starting quarterback Kemp and his Buffalo Bills. In 1964, San Diego fell 20–7. The following year, the Bills shut out the Chargers 23–0.

Behind the scenes, Hilton was working on two projects. His first task was a new stadium for his Chargers, since Balboa Stadium was outdated. By 1965, Hilton had raised $27 million, or about $270 million in 2024 money, for a new stadium. Opening in 1967, the Chargers' new home was called San Diego Stadium.

Quarterback John Hadl threw for 2,253 yards in 1969.

Hilton was also working to help the AFL join the NFL. Throughout the early 1960s, the leagues frequently fought over players. Owners of both leagues thought it would be best for the two to work together. With Hilton's assistance, the AFL and NFL agreed to merge. The leagues would officially join in the 1970 season, but starting with the 1966 season their champions met in a game that is now known as the Super Bowl.

The Chargers were a powerhouse team before the merger. However, they began to slip in the second half of the 1960s. Hadl was still a productive quarterback. He twice led the league in passing yards. Alworth was on his way to more than 500 career receptions. But Lowe had lost a step, and other original Chargers moved on or retired.

The team had winning records every year from 1963 to 1969 but never finished higher than third in the AFL's West Division. During the 1969 season, Gillman stepped down due to health concerns. The Chargers' success seemed to walk out the door with him. In 1970, the team's first season in the new American Football Conference (AFC) after the merger, the Chargers suffered a losing record for just the second time in their history.

JACK MURPHY

After the Chargers' poorly attended first season in Los Angeles, Jack Murphy lobbied Barron Hilton to move the team to San Diego. Murphy was a sportswriter and editor for the *San Diego Union*. When Hilton needed a new stadium five years later, Murphy wrote columns to campaign for one. After Murphy died in 1980, San Diego Stadium was renamed Jack Murphy Stadium. However, when the stadium's naming rights were sold in 1997, it became Qualcomm Stadium.

Future Hall of Fame quarterback Johnny Unitas threw for just 471 yards in 1973.

CHAPTER 3

AIR CORYELL

THE CHARGERS SUFFERED THROUGH A THIRD STRAIGHT LOSING SEASON IN 1972. The team's head coach/general manager Harland Svare decided to shake things up. Wanting some star power, he traded for legendary quarterback Johnny Unitas.

Unitas had been one of the league's all-time best passers over 17 seasons playing for the Baltimore Colts. But at 40 years old, he was no longer a great player. In five games with the Chargers, Unitas threw three touchdown passes and seven interceptions.

The Chargers thought they had their new star in rookie Dan Fouts, but the 22-year-old quarterback didn't play much better. The Chargers struggled to more losing records, including 2–12 in 1975. By the start of the 1978 season, Fouts had 34 career touchdown passes and 57 interceptions.

Quarterback Dan Fouts was the Chargers' third-round draft pick in 1973 after a record-setting college career at Oregon.

GOING VERTICAL

After starting 1–4 in 1978, Chargers owner Gene Klein hired a new head coach. Don Coryell was already well-known in San Diego. He had coached at San Diego State from 1961 to 1972 before working with the NFL's St. Louis Cardinals. Similar to Sid Gillman, Coryell was innovative and favored passing.

Coryell designed a system that gave players choices. On any play, the quarterback could assess the defense and decide at the line of scrimmage exactly where receivers should go. The offense also often shifted its formation before plays to confuse defenders. In addition, Coryell's offense used tight ends as receivers. In the early days of football, tight ends were mainly blockers. Under Coryell, they became weapons in his deep passing attack.

While Gillman had emphasized the passing game, Coryell modernized it. His passing strategy became known as "Air Coryell." Today, many NFL plays are influenced by Coryell.

Operating in Coryell's offense, Fouts transformed. The big-bearded, cannon-armed quarterback was perfect for the system. He also had help from sure-handed, speedy receivers Charlie Joiner and John Jefferson.

After the Chargers finished 9–7 in 1978 and just missed the playoffs, Coryell added another weapon to the team. San Diego drafted tight end Kellen Winslow, who was as fast as most receivers. With their offense set, the Chargers went 12–4 and won the AFC West in 1979.

Fouts became the second pro quarterback to ever top 4,000 yards passing. However, the quarterback had a rough playoff debut against the Houston Oilers. In the divisional round, he was intercepted five times in a 17–14 loss.

The following season, the Chargers added tough running back Chuck Muncie to boost the ground game and balance out the offense.

Don Coryell had a record of 69–56 in his nine seasons with the Chargers.

Suddenly San Diego's passing game was even more dangerous. Fouts threw for an NFL-record 4,715 yards. Jefferson, Joiner, and Winslow all topped 1,000 receiving yards.

After claiming the AFC West again, the Chargers faced the Buffalo Bills in the divisional round. With the Chargers trailing 14–3, Fouts rallied the team to 14–13. In the fourth quarter, he threw a 50-yard bomb to little-used receiver Ron Smith. The receiver grabbed the touchdown pass, and the Chargers won the game 20–14.

The following week, the Chargers battled the division rival Oakland Raiders in the AFC title game. The Chargers quickly fell

Fouts unleashes a pass during a game in 1980.

behind 28–7. San Diego rallied in the second half but fell short. The Chargers lost 34–27.

PLAYOFF EXTREMES

Before the 1981 season, Jefferson and defensive lineman Fred Dean wanted to renegotiate their contracts with Klein. The San Diego owner refused and traded the athletes. Then the team replaced Jefferson with former New Orleans Saints standout Wes Chandler, and the Chargers remained a passing machine. Fouts threw for a record 4,802 yards and an NFL-best 33 touchdowns as San Diego finished 10–6.

Receiver John Jefferson was known for his athletic catches during his time with the Chargers.

San Diego traveled to Miami for a divisional-round matchup against the Dolphins. With humidity heavy in the air and the temperature at 79 degrees Fahrenheit (26°C), it was difficult for players to compete. Even with their energy sapped, the players put on one of the most memorable playoff games in history.

Chargers kicker Rolf Benirschke began the scoring with a 32-yard field goal. The Chargers then added three touchdowns before the end of the first quarter to lead 24–0. But the Dolphins mounted a furious rally. The game turned into a shootout between Fouts

Chargers receiver Wes Chandler, *center*, celebrates his punt return touchdown against the Miami Dolphins during the teams' playoff matchup on January 2, 1982.

and Miami quarterback Don Strock. With less than five minutes remaining in the game, Miami held a 38–31 lead and had the ball.

On a running play, Chargers defensive tackle Louie Kelcher stripped the ball, and San Diego recovered it at its own 18. That gave the Chargers one last chance to tie the game. Fouts drove San Diego down the field to Miami's 9. With 1:07 remaining, he took the snap. Then Fouts threw a pass into the end zone that sailed over Winslow's head. But Brooks was running behind the tight end and caught the errant pass for a touchdown.

Benirschke's extra point tied the game. Miami then scrambled down the field and got into position for a would-be winning kick. The 6-foot-5-inch Winslow burst through the line and blocked it, forcing overtime.

In overtime, Benirschke missed a 27-yard attempt. The Chargers blocked another Miami attempt. Fouts then drove the Chargers to the Miami 10. Given a second chance, Benirschke nailed the winner to end "the Epic in Miami."

Rookie running back James Brooks had 525 rushing yards and caught 46 passes during the 1981 season.

The game was filled with memorable performances. But Winslow stood out from the crowd. Fighting through cramps and dehydration for most of the second half, the tight end set a playoff record with 13 receptions in addition to his key field-goal block. Many consider it one of the greatest individual performances in NFL playoff history. "I've coached for 31 or 32 years, and this is tremendous," Coryell said after the game. "There has never been another game like this. It was probably the most exciting game in pro football history."

> **"IT WAS PROBABLY THE MOST EXCITING GAME IN PRO FOOTBALL HISTORY."**
>
> **—DON CORYELL**

One week later, the Chargers traveled to Cincinnati to take on the Bengals in the AFC title game. San Diego went from one extreme to another. The game-time temperature was –9 degrees Fahrenheit (–23°C). The swirling wind made the temperature feel as if it were –59 degrees (–51°C). The game became known as "the Freezer Bowl."

The frigid weather halted the Chargers and their aerial attacks. In the second quarter, the Bengals were up 10-0. Fouts threw a pass to Winslow at the line of scrimmage, and the tight end took the ball 33 yards to the end zone. But San Diego failed to score again, and the Bengals won 27-7.

Chargers running back Chuck Muncie (46) loses a fumble during "the Freezer Bowl" on January 10, 1982.

RECORD SETTERS

A players' strike shortened the 1982 season to nine games. After finishing 6-3, the Chargers again faced off against Miami in the divisional round. This time it wasn't close, as the Dolphins rolled the Chargers 34-13.

Coryell stayed on as coach for another three and a half years but never coached the Chargers to another winning record. In 1984, Joiner caught his 650th career pass to set an NFL record. A year later, veteran Ed White broke the NFL record for offensive linemen by playing in his 241st game. That same year, versatile running back Lionel "Little Train" James totaled 1,027 receiving yards, the most ever by a running back. He also set an NFL mark with 2,535 all-purpose yards.

Coryell ended his coaching career eight games into the 1986 season. After the following season, Fouts retired. He told reporters that his 36-year-old body couldn't take the physical demands of being an NFL quarterback. A knee injury forced Winslow to retire before the 1988 season. All three were later inducted into the Hall of Fame. Both players credited Coryell for their success. Coryell's tactics changed football and gave San Diego one of the most exciting eras in NFL history. However, as the Chargers looked forward to the 1990s, they were starting over.

Receiver Charlie Joiner leaps to make a 20-yard reception in 1986. On the play, he broke the NFL record for career receiving yards.

THE HOLY ROLLER

In 1978, the Chargers lost to the Oakland Raiders on a bizarre last-second play. Oakland quarterback Ken Stabler fumbled near the Chargers' 20-yard line, but he intentionally tossed the ball forward. Another teammate did the same, and tight end Dave Casper kicked the ball toward the end zone and recovered it for a touchdown. "The Holy Roller" clinched a 21–20 victory for the Raiders. After the season, the NFL changed its rules. Then only the player who fumbled could advance the ball on fourth down and in the last two minutes of a half.

Chargers linebacker Junior Seau was inducted into the Pro Football Hall of Fame in 2015.

CHAPTER 4

SUPER CHARGERS

THE 1989 SEASON WAS THE CHARGERS' SECOND IN A ROW FINISHING 6-10. With the fifth pick in the next year's draft, general manager Bobby Beathard selected Junior Seau. The linebacker had grown up in nearby Oceanside, California, before starring at USC.

Seau was a dominant force. On the field, he terrified opponents with his speed and tough hits. His enthusiasm and incredible work ethic rubbed off on fans and teammates. Chargers defensive back Rodney Harrison once asked Seau why he practiced so hard. Seau responded, "Rodney, I get paid to practice. I play the game for free."

> **"I GET PAID TO PRACTICE. I PLAY THE GAME FOR FREE."**
>
> **—JUNIOR SEAU**

While Seau's play earned him the nickname "Tasmanian Devil," he was kind and gentle off the field. He carved out time for fans, especially children. Seau's dedication and local ties made him a San Diego icon.

After two strong seasons, Seau broke out as one of the NFL's best defensive players in 1992. That year, the Chargers also hired Bobby Ross as their new head coach and traded for veteran quarterback Stan Humphries. Altogether, they helped the Chargers achieve their best season in a decade.

Seau recorded 102 tackles while finishing second in the Defensive Player of the Year voting. Humphries threw for more than 3,300 yards. He often connected with versatile running back Ronnie Harmon and receiver Anthony Miller. Meanwhile, Ross, a former US Army officer, brought his strong sense of discipline to the team.

Seau, *right*, reached the Pro Bowl every season from 1991 to 2002, his final season in San Diego.

Quarterback Stan Humphries unleashes a pass against the Kansas City Chiefs in 1994.

With an 11–5 record, the Chargers won their division and reached the playoffs for the first time in 10 years. San Diego's defense was on full display in the wild-card round against the Kansas City Chiefs. During the regular season, defensive ends Leslie O'Neal and Chris Mims had combined for a total of 27 sacks. The Chargers kept it up as they sacked Kansas City quarterback Dave Krieg seven times in a 17–0 shutout. However, San Diego's season ended the next week with a 31–0 loss to the Miami Dolphins.

COMEBACK KIDS

On the opening day of the 1994 season, San Diego defensive back Stanley Richard intercepted Denver's John Elway and raced 99 yards for a touchdown. The pick six kicked off a thrilling season for the Chargers. In Week 3, Humphries and receiver Tony Martin pulled off a 99-yard scoring pass. As the season went on, returner Andre Coleman brought two kickoffs back for touchdowns. Darrien Gordon did the same on a pair of punt returns. San Diego ended the 1994 season with 10 scoring plays of 50 yards or more.

The 1994 Chargers defense was also stacked. Seau piled up 155 tackles, while O'Neal and Mims combined for a total of 23 1/2 sacks. San Diego held opponents to 19.1 points per game and won the AFC West again.

San Diego opened the playoffs in the divisional round against the Dolphins. In the first half, the Chargers struggled to contain Dolphins quarterback Dan Marino. The superstar threw three touchdown passes to give Miami a 21–6 lead.

However, a late third-quarter safety sparked a comeback. Soon after, San Diego's 245-pound

Defensive back Stanley Richard tied for the San Diego team lead with four interceptions in 1994. He returned two of them for touchdowns.

Running back Natrone Means rushed for 1,350 yards in 1994, which was a Chargers record at the time.

tailback Natrone Means rushed for 24 yards while dragging two Dolphins defenders the final 5 yards as he reached the end zone. Means's score made it 21–15. In the final minute of the fourth quarter, Humphries hit receiver Mark Seay on an 8-yard touchdown pass to seal San Diego's 22–21 comeback win.

The underdog Chargers traveled to Pittsburgh to take on the Steelers in the AFC Championship Game. Playing in the cold rain, San Diego's offense suffered. The team trailed 13–3 with just over eight minutes left in the third quarter when Humphries came alive. He fired a 43-yard touchdown pass to tight end Alfred Pupunu. With 5:13 left in the game, Humphries lobbed a 43-yard scoring bomb to Martin. That gave San Diego a 17–13 lead.

Pittsburgh mounted one last drive. With 1:09 left, the Steelers faced fourth-and-goal at the San Diego 3-yard line.

Quarterback Neil O'Donnell dropped back and threw a low pass over the middle. Chargers linebacker Dennis Gibson dived in front of a Steelers receiver and knocked the ball to the ground. San Diego clinched its first Super Bowl appearance.

COMING UP SHORT

Before San Diego faced its toughest test in Super Bowl XXIX, the National Football Conference (NFC) title game had featured the two-time defending champion Dallas Cowboys and the San Francisco 49ers. San Francisco had won four championships since the 1981 season. In a slight to the Chargers and Steelers, the media had hyped up the NFC title game as "the real Super Bowl." Most expected the 49ers to roll over the Chargers when they met in Miami.

Linebacker Dennis Gibson celebrates after his game-sealing pass deflection in the 1994 AFC title game.

The Super Bowl could not have started any worse for San Diego. On the 49ers' third offensive play, quarterback Steve Young hit legendary wide receiver Jerry Rice on a 44-yard touchdown pass over the middle. During the fourth play of San Francisco's next drive, Young found running back Ricky Watters on a 51-yard strike to make the score 14–0.

Late in the first quarter, the Chargers' offense settled in. Means capped off a 13-play drive with a 1-yard touchdown run, cutting San Francisco's lead in half. But the San Diego defense couldn't contain the 49ers' exceptional passing game. Before halftime, Young threw two more touchdown passes. San Diego could only counter with a field goal from kicker John Carney and trailed 28–10 at the break.

In the third quarter, San Francisco's lead grew to 42–10. With 7:25 left in that quarter, Coleman delivered the Chargers' biggest Super Bowl XXIX highlight. Grabbing a kickoff at the 2-yard line, the wide receiver sprinted up the left sideline 98 yards for a touchdown. It was the first kickoff return for a score in a Super Bowl since 1989. However, the Chargers' celebration was short-lived. Young ended the game with a Super Bowl-record six touchdown passes as San Diego fell 49–26.

Andre Coleman sprints down the sideline for his kickoff return touchdown in Super Bowl XXIX on January 29, 1995.

A NEW LEAF

After starting the 1995 season 4–7, the Chargers rallied to win their final five games and clinched a second consecutive playoff spot. However, their season ended abruptly with a 35-20 loss to the underdog Indianapolis Colts in the wild-card round. As the season ended, so did the Chargers' short run of success.

Bobby Ross had a record of 47-33 in five seasons as the Chargers' head coach.

After the Chargers missed the playoffs the following year, Ross resigned. Under new coach Kevin Gilbride, San Diego stumbled to a 4-12 record in 1997. Humphries, beaten up by years of hard hits, retired due to his injuries. San Diego entered the 1998 NFL Draft in need of a quarterback.

The draft's top two prospects, Tennessee's Peyton Manning and Washington State's Ryan Leaf, were both quarterbacks. At the time, opinion was split as to who was going to be the better player. What was certain was that the Indianapolis Colts would take one of the quarterbacks with the first overall pick. San Diego traded up one spot to the second pick. After the Colts selected Manning first, the Chargers gladly grabbed Leaf.

Leaf had a cannon of a right arm and had put up huge numbers with the Cougars. Scouts loved his toughness as well.

However, some questioned whether he was mature enough to lead an NFL team. The Chargers quickly found out that those scouts' concerns were right. Baffled by complicated defenses in the professional game, Leaf threw only two touchdowns and 15 interceptions as a rookie. He showed a poor attitude during the process. After his third game, a reporter asked him about his struggles. Leaf responded by screaming at the writer. Teammates had to lead the quarterback away.

Leaf lasted just three seasons with the Chargers, including one that he missed with a shoulder injury. His final totals with the team were 13 touchdowns and 33 interceptions. The Chargers had a record of only 4–14 in games Leaf started. After the 2000 season, the Chargers let Leaf go. Beathard, who drafted Leaf, retired that offseason as well. Six years after reaching the Super Bowl, the Chargers had hit rock bottom and needed to make huge changes.

SAN DIEGO SUPER CHARGERS

In 1979, Chargers owner Gene Klein asked two local musicians to write the team a theme song that would be played when the team scored. The result was a disco song called "San Diego Super Chargers" by a band called Captain Q. B. and the Big Boys. Ten years later, new owner Alex Spanos created a new version of the song. In 2002, Alex's son Dean revived the original to be played at games.

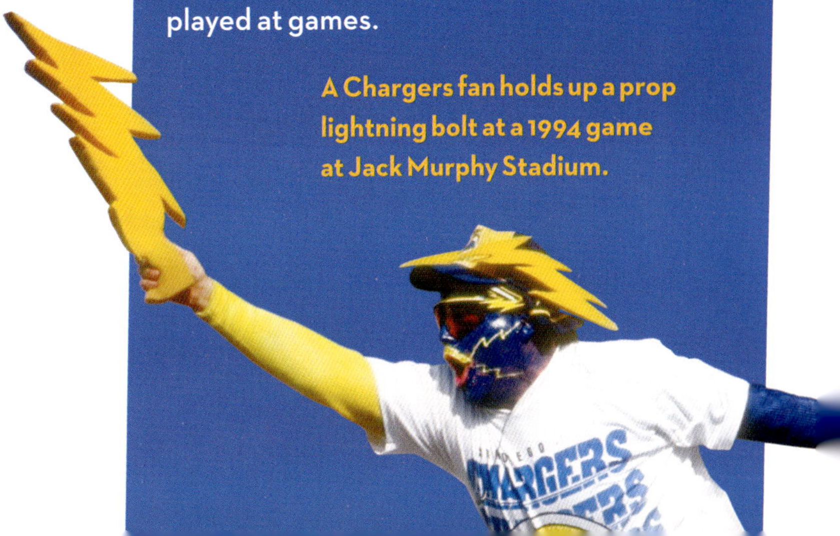

A Chargers fan holds up a prop lightning bolt at a 1994 game at Jack Murphy Stadium.

Chargers running back LaDainian Tomlinson rushed 36 times for 113 yards and two touchdowns in his NFL debut.

CHAPTER 5

RETURN TO LOS ANGELES

AFTER A 1–15 SEASON IN 2000, THE CHARGERS HAD NOWHERE TO go but up. The team entered the 2001 draft with the top pick. New general manager John Butler had a big decision to make, and what he did shocked the NFL.

The top prospect that year was electrifying quarterback Michael Vick. A player who could run as well as he could throw, Vick was a rare athlete. However, the Chargers and Vick couldn't agree on contract terms. So, Butler decided to trade the top pick to the Atlanta Falcons, who had the fifth spot. Atlanta took Vick, and Butler selected running back LaDainian Tomlinson.

Vick indeed became a star. But the bet also paid off for the Chargers, as Tomlinson burst onto the NFL scene by rushing for 1,236 yards and

10 touchdowns as a rookie. Only one Charger had ever rushed for more yards in a season.

The next year, the Chargers hired coach Marty Schottenheimer, who loved the running game. Tomlinson thrived in the team's new system. The quiet running back known as "L. T." shattered the team record by rushing for 1,683 yards.

PLAYOFF DISAPPOINTMENT

Tomlinson's excellence helped the Chargers improve. Quarterback Drew Brees, who arrived in the second round of the 2001 draft, blossomed into a Pro Bowl passer in 2004. That season, he had a new receiving weapon that the Chargers found in an unconventional place.

Quarterback Drew Brees (9) reached the Pro Bowl once in his five seasons with the Chargers.

Antonio Gates never played college football. Instead, he had been a standout basketball player at Kent State. But Gates had played football in high school, and the Chargers thought his athletic ability made him a good fit as a tight end. They picked up Gates as an undrafted rookie free agent in 2003. After a solid rookie year, Gates exploded in 2004 with 81 catches for 964 yards and 13 touchdowns. It was the start of an incredible 16-year career in which Gates set Chargers receiving records for catches, yards, and touchdowns.

Tight end Antonio Gates shows off his basketball skills by dunking the ball over the crossbar after a touchdown in 2004.

That star trio of Brees, Gates, and Tomlinson helped San Diego win the AFC West with a 12–4 record in 2004. However, with Tomlinson held in check, the Chargers fell behind the New York Jets 17–7 entering the fourth quarter of their wild-card round game. Kicker Nate Kaeding got three points back on a field goal. San Diego needed a touchdown to tie the game. The team got just that when Brees connected with Gates for a 1-yard touchdown pass with 11 seconds left in the game. In overtime, Brees led an eight-minute, 13-play drive to the New York 22. Kaeding had a chance to win it with a field goal. But the rookie's kick swerved right, and the Jets eventually won 20–17.

DRAFT DAY DRAMA

The Chargers held the top pick in the 2004 NFL Draft. The top prospect was Eli Manning, the younger brother of Peyton Manning. However, Eli had no desire to play in San Diego and told the Chargers not to draft him. San Diego did anyway, but quickly traded him to the New York Giants for Philip Rivers, whom New York had taken with the fourth overall pick.

The careers of Eli Manning, *left*, and Philip Rivers, *right*, have always been linked due to the 2004 trade involving both players.

RECORD RUNS

Brees had shown promise in San Diego. However, he seriously injured his shoulder during the 2005 season and no one was sure how he'd recover. So after missing the playoffs in 2005, the Chargers elected to start over and didn't re-sign Brees, who joined the New Orleans Saints. It also helped that the Chargers had a top quarterback prospect ready to go. In a 2004 draft-day trade, San Diego had picked up young quarterback Philip Rivers. By 2006,

Tomlinson, *left*, was named both the NFL's Offensive Player of the Year and MVP in 2006.

the third-year player was ready to take over. Rivers threw with an unconventional sidearm style, but he got results. In his first year as a starter, he threw for more than 3,000 yards.

Tomlinson was a workhorse running back. With his involvement in both running and passing plays, he often had the ball. In 2006, he had 404 touches. That same year, Tomlinson rushed for a career-high 1,815 yards and caught 56 passes for 506 more. But what set his season apart was how many times he found the end zone. The superstar set an NFL record with 28 rushing touchdowns. With three more through the air, Tomlinson also set a league mark with 31 total scores. Opponents were in awe of the Chargers' star. Baltimore Ravens linebacker Ray Lewis said of Tomlinson, "It was almost impossible to defend him . . . because he had hands like a

Tomlinson scores a touchdown against the New England Patriots in the playoffs after the 2006 season.

receiver, he had feet like a ballet dancer, and had a heart like a lion."

"HE HAD HANDS LIKE A RECEIVER, HE HAD FEET LIKE A BALLET DANCER, AND HAD A HEART LIKE A LION."

—RAY LEWIS

The Chargers finished with the best record in team history at 14–2. As a reward, they got to host the powerhouse New England Patriots in the divisional playoffs. New England had won three Super Bowls in the previous five years. The Chargers weren't intimidated, though. After Tomlinson's second touchdown of the game, San Diego had a 21–13 lead in the fourth quarter. With just over six minutes left, Chargers defensive back Marlon McCree intercepted New England quarterback Tom Brady at the Chargers' 31. But after taking a few steps, McCree fumbled, and the Patriots got the ball back. Given a second chance, Brady led a touchdown drive, and a two-point conversion tied the game. New England then won it on a field goal with 1:10 left.

A year later, the two teams met in the AFC Championship Game. The Chargers were one step from the Super Bowl for the first time since the 1994 season. But they were playing shorthanded. Rivers had a torn ligament in his knee. He played on his injured leg and completed only 19 of 37 passes. He also threw two interceptions. Meanwhile, Tomlinson

Eric Weddle was an All-Pro safety twice for the Chargers.

also became injured early in the game and watched the rest from the sideline. Without their offensive stars healthy, the Chargers lost 21–12.

BACK WHERE IT STARTED

Though the Chargers went back to the playoffs in both the 2008 and 2009 seasons, they didn't get past the divisional round. And by the end of 2009, the team's star running back was worn out from his heavy workload. Tomlinson rushed for under 1,000 yards that season for the first time in his career. The Chargers let him go that offseason.

Rivers was on his way to breaking Dan Fouts's team passing records, and Gates was still a star in the early 2010s, but they weren't enough for San Diego to be a contender. The team reached the divisional playoffs in 2013. Despite a spirited fourth-quarter comeback after being down 17–0, the Chargers lost 24–17 to the Denver Broncos.

The biggest news for the Chargers was happening off the field. Since 1967, the team had been playing in the same stadium. The building known as Qualcomm Stadium needed to be replaced. Owner Dean Spanos had been trying to get the local government to help build a new home for years. After falling short in those efforts, he was ready to move the team in 2015. The Chargers asked the NFL if they could move back to Los Angeles, where they had first played in 1960. The league agreed, and more than 50 years of football history in San Diego came to an end when the Chargers moved in 2017.

Defensive end Joey Bosa, *right*, was named the NFL's Defensive Rookie of the Year in 2016 after recording 10 1/2 sacks on the season.

Rivers topped 4,000 passing yards 11 times in 16 seasons with the Chargers.

Rivers moved with the team and led the once-again Los Angeles Chargers to a playoff berth in 2018. The Chargers beat the Ravens in the wild-card round. But the team again fell short against the Patriots in the divisional round.

After one more season in 2019, the 38-year-old Rivers left the Chargers as a free agent. He had 59,271 career passing yards, which was more than 16,000 ahead of Fouts's old team record. Rivers also tossed 397 touchdowns with the team.

Wide receiver Keenan Allen reached the Pro Bowl six times in 11 seasons playing for the Chargers.

The Chargers moved on from Rivers and needed a new quarterback. Los Angeles drafted Justin Herbert from Oregon, where Fouts had played. Herbert immediately excelled. In Herbert's second season, Brandon Staley became the team's new head coach. The quarterback combined with star receiver Keenan Allen to pace the offense. Pass rusher Joey Bosa and

CHARGERS TROPHY CASE

SUPER BOWL CHAMPIONSHIPS: 0

CONFERENCE CHAMPIONSHIPS: 1

1994

AFL CHAMPIONSHIPS: 1

1963

DIVISION TITLES: 15

AFL West: 1960, 1961, 1963, 1964, 1965
AFC West: 1979, 1980, 1981, 1992, 1994, 2004, 2006, 2007, 2008, 2009

All stats are through the 2024 season.

thumping defensive back Derwin James led Los Angeles's defense. In 2022, the team finished 10-7 and headed back to the playoffs.

The team's postseason stay was disastrous. Los Angeles built a 27-0 lead in the first half of its wild-card game against the

Defensive back Derwin James reached the Pro Bowl in 2024.

Jim Harbaugh, *right*, talks to Justin Herbert during the Chargers' 2024 season opener against the Las Vegas Raiders.

Jacksonville Jaguars. Then the Chargers dried up, and Jacksonville stormed back for a 31–30 victory. It was the third-largest playoff collapse in NFL history.

The playoff meltdown left fans questioning Staley as head coach. And when the team struggled in 2023, the calls for his replacement became louder. Staley was eventually let go after an embarrassing 63–21 loss to the Las Vegas Raiders in Week 15.

Before the 2024 season, the Chargers made a splashy coaching hire by bringing in Jim Harbaugh. The former Chargers quarterback had played for the team from 1999 to 2000. He later became a renowned coach, leading the San Francisco 49ers to a Super Bowl appearance and Michigan to a collegiate national championship. The Chargers hired him in 2024, hoping he could bring those winning ways to Los Angeles. Harbaugh got off to a strong start, lifting the team to an 11–6 record and back into the playoffs. Despite Chargers receiver Ladd McConkey setting a rookie playoff record with 197 receiving yards, the Houston Texans beat Los Angeles 32–12. While another season ended in heartbreak, Chargers fans still believed Harbaugh could lead the team to the top.

TIMELINE

1960
The Chargers are founded in Los Angeles and reach the AFL title game in their first season.

1961
After moving to San Diego, the Chargers set professional records for forced turnovers and interceptions while reaching the AFL title game again.

1964
On January 5, the Chargers win their first AFL title by beating the Boston Patriots 51–10 after the 1963 season.

1965
On December 26, the Chargers reach the AFL title game for the third consecutive season but lose to the Buffalo Bills for the second straight year.

1973
Dan Fouts makes his Chargers debut after taking over for veteran Johnny Unitas.

1979
Fouts becomes the second pro quarterback to pass for more than 4,000 yards in a season as the Chargers win the AFC West.

1981
On January 11, the Chargers reach the AFC title game but lose to the Oakland Raiders 34–27 after the 1980 season.

1982
After winning "the Epic in Miami," the Chargers lose the AFC title game to the Cincinnati Bengals in "the Freezer Bowl" on January 10, after the 1981 season.

1988
Fouts retires as the Chargers' all-time leading passer.

1992
The Chargers make the playoffs for the first time in 10 years.

1995
San Diego reaches Super Bowl XXIX after the 1994 season but loses to the San Francisco 49ers 49–26.

2006
Running back LaDainian Tomlinson sets an NFL record by scoring 31 touchdowns in a season.

2017
The Chargers move back to Los Angeles.

2020
Quarterback Justin Herbert sets a rookie record by throwing 31 touchdown passes in a season.

GLOSSARY

contender–a person or team that has a good chance at winning a championship.

contract–an agreement to play for a certain team.

draft–a system that allows teams to acquire new players coming into the league.

franchise–an entire sports organization.

free agent–a player who is not signed to a team.

general manager–an executive who runs a team and is responsible for finding and signing players.

icon–a player who is well known for excellence.

innovative–having new ideas about how something can be done.

lobby–to argue on behalf of a cause or idea.

merge–join with another to create something new, such as a company, a team, or a league.

pick six–an interception returned for a touchdown.

players' strike– a work stoppage due to a disagreement between players and their employers (teams) about things such as working conditions or wages.

prospect–an athlete likely to succeed at the next level.

rival–an opponent with whom a player or team has a fierce and ongoing competition.

rookie–a professional athlete in his or her first year of competition.

sack—a tackle of the quarterback behind the line of scrimmage before he can pass the ball.

safety—a score of two points for a team when its opponent is unable to advance the ball out of its own end zone.

tactic—a carefully planned action or strategy.

underdog—the person or team that is not expected to win.

versatile—able to perform many different roles or functions.

ONLINE RESOURCES

Booklinks
NONFICTION NETWORK
FREE! ONLINE NONFICTION RESOURCES

To learn more about the Los Angeles Chargers, please visit **abdobooklinks.com** or scan this QR code. These links are routinely monitored and updated to provide the most current information available.

INDEX